April 29, 2001

Dear Kathy,

Congratulations on your graduation

I pray that the blessing of the Lord Make you Rich and with it he will add no sorrow.

I pray for clarity in God's direction for your life and that spirit of wisdom and revelation in the knowledge of Christ would rest heavenly upon you.

God bless you

Shal preschool Director

Published by Barbour Publishing, Inc., P.O. Box 719, Uhrichsville, Ohio 44683
http://www.barbourbooks.com

Member of the
Evangelical Christian
Publishers Association

Printed in China.

Wisdom

FOR THE GRADUATE

Colleen L. Reece
Julie Reece-DeMarco

PUBLISHING, INC.

INTRODUCTION

Tools are gifts from God that enable us to do things our ordinary strength will not permit. They make formidable tasks simple. Without tools, we would not have shelter, heat, food, entertainment, or other basic necessities of life.

Just as God has provided tools for living, He has also given each of us tools to use in finding our way and achieving our goals. Unfortunately, we don't always recognize that we have them!

Consider Tom, who for years had longed to serve God. Yet the painful shyness he fought since childhood made his dream seem impossible. How could he become a minister when the thought of speaking in front of others terrified him?

As Tom earnestly prayed for strength to accomplish his goals, he felt God whisper in his soul, "You have the strength." Those few words gave Tom the tool to overcome his fears. Thankful and encouraged, he realized his deepest dream and became a minister.

Many years later Tom realized the strength he desperately needed had not—as he initially assumed—arrived while he prayed. God's reassurance, "You *have* the strength," didn't refer to a gift God was bestowing upon Tom, but to an undiscovered reservoir of strength Tom wasn't aware he already possessed.

Are you like Tom, afraid to pursue your life's dreams? Are you still finding your way, unsure of yourself and your gifts? This book can help you recognize and use your God-given tools.

A Bag of Tools

Isn't it strange that princes and kings,
And clowns that caper in sawdust rings,
And common people like you and me
Are builders for eternity?

Each is given a bag of tools,
A shapeless mass, a book of rules;
And each must make—ere life is flown—
A stumbling block or a steppingstone.

R. L. Sharpe

PART 1

Using Tools Passed Down through Generations

The words of the great poet Henry Wadsworth Longfellow challenge every generation:

> Lives of great men all remind us
> We can make our lives sublime,
> And, departing, leave behind us
> Footprints on the sands of time.

Sometimes our choices leave more than just footprints, as in this story told of Mahatma Gandhi, the social reformer who helped free India from British rule by advocating nonviolent resistance, including prolonged fasting. Once, running alongside a moving train, Gandhi leaped aboard but lost a shoe in the process. He snatched off his other shoe and flung it out of the train.

A gaping fellow traveler demanded, "Why did you do that?"

Gandhi smiled. "Now the one who finds my shoe will have a pair."

Using our given tools for the benefit of ourselves and others often requires great effort. The old adage "We only get out of life what we put into it" rings true. Taking a stand contrary to popular opinion and speaking out for our beliefs is seldom easy. Accomplishing great things in this life requires hard work and dedication. Our decisions and commitment to our goals not only profoundly affect our own lives, but may change the course of human events.

Reflect on these individuals whose commitment to follow a different path has been admirable.

* *Mother Teresa,* internationally acclaimed humanitarian, left her convent to work one-on-one with the poor, downtrodden, and forgotten people of Calcutta, India. Her decision to serve thousands of miles away from her Yugoslavian birthplace in a land without the comforts of home resulted in years of compassionate ministry. It earned her the title "Saint of the Gutters," as well as the Nobel Peace Prize.

> *I was hungry and you gave me something to eat,*
> *I was thirsty. . .you gave me something to drink. . .*
> *I needed clothes. . .you clothed me. . .*
> *I was sick. . .you looked after me.*
> MATTHEW 25:35–36 NIV

* *A. C. Green,* a 6'9" pro basketball player, refused to allow locker-room boasts about sexual conquests to weaken his resolve to remain sexually pure, quoting Philippians 4:13 (NIV): *"I can do everything through him* [Christ] *who gives me strength."* Green has spoken out to young people that not everyone is "doing it," and he has promoted secondary

virginity for those already sexually active. One wonders how many lives may be changed because Green was true to himself and God.

- *Dan Quayle,* former vice president of the United States, was asked in a televised debate what he would do if he were in office and the president suddenly became incapacitated. Quayle replied, "First I'd say a prayer." Opponents had a field day with his answer, but their reaction raised a question: What answer would better serve our country?

> *My help comes from the LORD,*
> *the Maker of heaven and earth.*
> PSALM 121:2 NIV

- *Harriet Tubman,* the famed abolitionist, risked prison and death in order to be true to herself. She received a skull fracture at age thirteen while courageously intervening to save a fellow slave from punishment. For the rest of her life Harriet suffered blackouts, but that didn't deter her from helping hundreds of slaves escape to free states and Canada. Neither was she deterred by the high price placed on her head by those who wished her dead. Countless persons were saved by the courage of this woman, heralded as a nineteenth-century Moses.

In all thy ways acknowledge him,
and he shall direct thy paths.
PROVERBS 3:6 KJV

- *Patrick Henry,* the famous orator and political leader
  during the Revolutionary War, risked charges of treason
  by urging the 1775 Virginia Provisional Convention to
  arm its militia to defend the colony against England.
  Henry is best remembered for his stirring words, "Give
  me liberty or give me death!"

Proclaim liberty to the captives.
ISAIAH 61:1 KJV

- *Candace and Kirk Cameron,* popular brother/sister TV
  stars, agree on the importance of saving one's self for
  marriage. Candace has flatly stated that she didn't intend
  to share the unique gift of sex with a bunch of people.
  Kirk and his wife, Chelsea Noble, did a *Focus on the*
  Family video, "Sex, Lies, and. . .The Truth," that aired on
  prime-time television. Kirk says, "I'm glad I waited."

Set an example. . .in life,
in love, . . .in purity.
1 TIMOTHY 4:12 NIV

- *Florence Nightingale,* considered the founder of modern nursing, shocked her wealthy English family by becoming a nurse at a time when hospital conditions were deplorable and nurses were often unfit to care for the sick. Countless soldiers in the Crimean War owed their lives to the "lady with the lamp" who badgered officials for desperately needed medical supplies, food, and bedding. Herself weak and ill from fever, but determined to change conditions—especially in military field hospitals—Nightingale insisted, "I can stand out the war with any man."

> *Your word is a lamp to my feet*
> *and a light for my path.*
> PSALM 119:105 NIV

- *John Newton,* the beloved hymn writer, came to Christ and bitterly repented of his years as a slave trader. Recognizing that even those who have not lived exemplary lives can change, he went on to touch the hearts of many by writing one of the world's most loved hymns. It begins:

> Amazing grace, how sweet the sound,
> That saved a wretch like me!
> I once was lost but now am found,
> Was blind but now I see.

- *Mary,* the earthly mother of Jesus, was young and unmarried when the angel Gabriel came to tell her she was chosen to bear the Son of God. Despite the scorn and whispered rumors in her small village, she stood and courageously testified of the angelic visit. Nine months pregnant, she braved the long, wilderness journey to the City of David, riding on the back of a donkey. Mary trusted and followed the direction of God despite her fears and discomfort. Because of her obedience and sacrifice, the Savior of the world was born in a stable in Bethlehem.

> *She* [Elizabeth] *exclaimed:*
> *"Blessed are you among women,*
> *and blessed is the child you will bear!"*
> LUKE 1:42 NIV

- *Viktor Frankl,* renowned author and psychiatrist, struggled through the loss of his wife and his imprisonment in a World War II concentration camp. Emerging from the darkness of that experience, he went on to publish a number of books on finding meaning in suffering and purpose in life. Frankl's writings have provided hope to many who have to overcome their own forms of suffering.

Bless those who curse you,
pray for those who mistreat you.
Luke 6:28 NIV

- *Jesus Christ,* the Son of God, chose the high road.
  Throughout His life, He exemplified the principles of
  goodness and righteousness. He spent years traversing
  the countryside, preaching to people He had never met.
  He continued to bring the same teachings even to audiences who found His message unpopular and made it
  the subject of much mocking and jest.

Jesus did not shrink from His duty in the face of ridicule. He told the
moneychangers they were doing wrong, even though it was *not* what
they wished to hear. He admonished those who would cast rocks at
the adulterous woman, challenging, "If any one of you is without sin,
let him be the first to throw a stone at her" (John 8:7 NIV).

He did not stop His work in the face of exhaustion. He did not
stop when His best friends betrayed him. Even when His adher-
ence to teaching the principles of righteousness ultimately led to
His death, still Jesus did not waver. He knew Whose work He was
doing. Kneeling in the Garden of Gethsemane, with sweat pouring
from His body like great drops of blood, still Jesus prayed, "Father,
if you are willing, take this cup from me; yet not my will, but yours
be done" (Luke 22:42 NIV).

Through pain, betrayal, ridicule, death, and a glorious Resurrection, Christ continued to be faithful. Because of His faithfulness, all those who have come after Him have not only the promise of the Atonement but a perfect example to look to for hope, direction, and guidance in finding their way.

THE LORD'S PRAYER

Our Father which art in heaven,
Hallowed be thy name.
Thy kingdom come.
Thy will be done in earth, as it is in heaven.
Give us this day our daily bread.
And forgive us our debts, as we forgive our debtors.
And lead us not into temptation,
but deliver us from evil:
For thine is the kingdom,
and the power, and the glory, for ever.
Amen.

MATTHEW 6:9–13 KJV

Part 2

A Pocketful of Tools

Most tools are designed for one purpose: A hammer pounds nails, a screwdriver loosens or tightens screws. But universal or "multi-tools" perform many different tasks. Spiritually speaking, the Ten Commandments might be considered among this latter group, for they have helped people in many ways for centuries. In today's language, here are these ten tools for living (Exodus 20):

- Have no other gods before the Lord God.
- Don't make idols of any kind; don't bow down and worship them.
- Never misuse the Lord's name.
- Keep the Sabbath holy.
- Honor your father and mother.
- Never murder anyone.
- Don't commit adultery.
- Don't steal.
- Don't give false testimony against others.
- Don't covet what isn't yours.

In the New Testament, Jesus provides two more spiritual "universal tools." Replying to the Pharisee lawyer who tried to trick Him by asking which was the greatest commandment, Jesus said, " 'Love the Lord your God with all your heart and with all your soul and with all your mind.' This is the first and greatest commandment. And the second is like it: 'Love your neighbor as yourself'" (Matthew 22:36–40 NIV).

Recognizing and using these words as tools will help you face many of life's challenges.

Other Valuable Tools

1. TOOLS TO HELP WITH SUCCESSFUL JOB INTERVIEWS
   - *Prepare ahead of time.*
     Research (talk with friends who have gone through the process).
     Learn the mission, policies, and focus of the company.
     Visualize yourself walking into the office, greeting the interviewer, and so on.
     Pray.

Alfred, Lord Tennyson wrote, *"More things are wrought by prayer than this world dreams of."*

     Proofread your résumé and cover letter.
     Read the job description carefully.
     Provide all materials required for the application.
     Practice questions and answers you may be asked or will ask.
     Review your greatest accomplishments and qualities.

- *Think about first impressions.*
  Wear comfortable, professional clothing.
  Avoid anything that distracts your attention from the
  interview.
  Check details: chipped nail polish, food on teeth,
  stained tie.
  Arrive on time. Take three deep breaths, hold, and slowly
  release before entering the office.
  Maintain good eye contact and expression of interest.

- *Be aware of your demeanor.*
  Avoid expressing potentially controversial opinions.
  Speak confidently if or when you're asked about goals.
  Avoid nervous habits, e.g., biting nails, twirling hair,
  blinking excessively, hand wringing, using verbal fillers
  such as "uh" and "um."
  Stick to answering the interviewer's questions.
  Answer questions honestly. Always put your best self
  forward.

Jim was surprised to be asked during an interview if he kept his car clean. He quickly responded, "Yes."

The interviewer then inquired when he washed it last.

"Yesterday," Jim replied.

To his amazement, the person conducting the interview quietly said, "Show me."

They went to the parking lot. Jim's car obviously hadn't been washed in some time. "Thank you for coming in," the interviewer said. "We won't be needing you."

2. TOOLS FOR MAINTAINING YOUR HEALTH

Leaving home for the first time brings a wealth of new experiences. Gaining new knowledge, friends, responsibility, and independence is often accompanied by other not so pleasant gains, like excess pounds and bad habits. Starting out on the right foot can be your key to developing positive and healthy habits for a lifetime.

- *Fuel your body.*
   Always eat *something* for breakfast. (Coffee doesn't qualify.)
   Keep healthful snacks in your dorm room or kitchen for when cravings hit.
   Eat frequent, smaller meals to avoid binging.
   Don't study or watch TV while eating. (It's amazing how many calories you can consume when you are distracted.)
   Choose foods wisely when eating out or in a school cafeteria to avoid the many high-fat, low-nutrition traps.
   Avoid putting harmful substances into your body.
   Carry a filled water bottle with you at all times to ensure you get plenty of fluids.

Do not let yourself get caught up in "comparing" your body with the bodies of your friends, movie stars, or magazine models. College campuses are breeding grounds for eating disorders. Remember, everyone has a different body type. Trying to drastically change yours can destroy your body or even kill you.

- *Exercise.*
  Participate in aerobic exercise at least three times per week.
  Choose to walk, not drive, to the store, campus, or friends' houses.
  Find opportunities to move around. For example, take the stairs, not elevators.
  Get involved with local or intramural sports teams.
  Take many short breaks from studying or working to stretch and walk.
  Plan social activities involving movement, e.g., scavenger hunts, outdoor games, dances.

- *Get plenty of sleep.*

3. TOOLS FOR ESTABLISHING FINANCIAL FREEDOM

"Danger. Tread Carefully" signs should accompany every new graduate's checkbook or credit card, not to mention those of people many years removed from college. Graduation often marks the start of financial independence and decision making. First-time check-books, credit cards, incoming bills, and temptations to buy can be traps leading to a lifetime of financial problems. Weekly offers of "preapprovals" for large amounts of cash are sent by credit card companies to unsuspecting students and graduates. Getting a grasp on the maze of financial pitfalls is easier when you remember the following:

- Record immediately every check you write in your checkbook and adjust the balance.
- Prepare a budget for an entire year, recording all known and anticipated monthly expenses on one side, and all guaranteed monthly income on the other. This will provide guidance on how much "extra" income you may have to spend for items you want. Adjust your budget every time there is a change in expenses or income.
- Always keep an emergency cash fund (for unexpected expenses) available in a savings account.
- Keep all your bills in one designated place and make sure you pay them on time. (Failure to pay bills on time when you are young may haunt your credit rating when you are older.)
- Tear up offers for "preapproved" credit cards immediately. If you can't afford to pay cash for an item, you probably can't afford to be paying interest on it.
- Read the fine print on the credit card application carefully; pay off each purchase before the end of the

       month to avoid accumulating large amounts of interest.

- Wait to make large purchases. If you still want an item after a week, then consider buying it. You'll be less likely to buy on impulse.
- Cut coupons and comparison shop to avoid paying more than necessary.
- Get help immediately if you find yourself in financial trouble. Parents, clergy, counselors, and free local consumer credit agencies can help.
- Put aside a small amount of money each month into a long-term savings account—and don't touch it.

4. TOOLS FOR GOOD DECISION-MAKING

Involve God on a daily basis. *"We should give God the same place in our hearts that He holds in the universe"* (Author unknown).

Gather all the information possible to make an informed decision.

Listen to others and consider their opinions carefully.

Make the decision that is right for *you*.

5. TOOLS FOR LEARNING TO ACCEPT RESPONSIBILITY

Each choice we make has consequences. Learning to accept responsibility for our decisions and actions is mandatory for success. A recent incident at the Puyallup (Washington) Fair illustrates this important aspect of achieving maturity.

After a morning exploring the fairgrounds, twenty-one-month-old Brianha and her grandfather paused to share a snack. Brianha neatly piled her fish-shaped crackers, then spilled them. She didn't cry. She didn't beg for more crackers. She simply bent over and picked up a few.

Her grandfather watched closely to make sure they didn't end up in her mouth, but Brianha didn't eat them. Instead, she trotted approximately ten feet to the closest garbage can, deposited her small handful, came back, and repeated her performance.

A curious crowd gathered, leaving room on the sidewalk for Brianha to make her journey back and forth, back and forth, until she disposed of a couple dozen spilled crackers, one or two at a time. "What's she doing?" several amazed newcomers wanted to know.

"Cleaning up her mess," the proud grandfather replied.

Brianha's example demonstrated every principle necessary when we appropriately accept responsibility for our choices and actions.

- She didn't waste time whining about her loss.
- She didn't blame others for what she had done.
- She didn't walk away from her mess or stand around waiting for someone else to come clean it up. She took action. Immediately.
- When a kind woman offered to help, Brianha shook her head and said, "No." It was her mess. She recognized it was her responsibility to handle it.

- Brianha faithfully worked until every trace of the problem lay in the garbage can where it belonged.

Several dozen adults left the Puyallup Fair with a special memory of the little girl faithfully carrying out her task, another confirmation of the Scripture, *"and a little child will lead them"* (Isaiah 11:6 NIV).

6. TOOLS FOR MAINTAINING SPIRITUALITY

Debbie had always been close to God. A leader in her church youth group, a dedicated member of the church choir, and a frequent volunteer in the community, she was a wonderful example to all those around her—until she left home to go to college. Tired from studying and late-night activities, Debbie stopped going to church. Her nightly prayers got shorter and shorter. Finally, they stopped.

Loneliness set in. Desperate to be accepted, Debbie clung to Sam, the only person who had shown her any kindness. Alone and confused, she did whatever she could to hold on to Sam, but to no avail. Pregnant and abandoned, Debbie wondered why this had happened to her.

Like Debbie, our choices help us to maintain or lose our spirituality. One string wrapped around our hand is easy to break. Twenty cannot be broken. Embarking on a new life filled with changes, challenges, and activities can distract us from noticing that Satan is systematically wrapping "strings" around us. It is important to remember and use those tools that can help us remain spiritually strong.

- Find a church close to your new home and make regular attendance a priority.
- Take time to pray and talk with God on a daily basis.
- Choose friends who inspire you to live a better life.

"A friend is a present you give yourself," wrote Robert Louis Stevenson.

John Evelyn identified friendship as *"the golden thread that ties the heart of all the world."*

- Choose social activities you wouldn't be embarrassed to attend with your parents, church friends, or pastor.
- Volunteer with a service organization in your new community.
- Read the Scriptures and other uplifting literature frequently.

"The Bible is a book in comparison with which all others are of minor importance, and which in all my perplexities and distresses has never failed to give me light and strength," Robert E. Lee said.

"I would rather be a poor man in a garret with plenty of books than a king who did not love reading," Thomas Macaulay wrote.

Charles Kingsley said, *"Except a living man there is nothing more wonderful than a book."*

PART 3

USING GOD'S TOOLS
TO BUILD YOUR DREAMS

I'd rather be the ship that sails
And rides the billows wild and free;
Than to be the ship that always fails
To leave its port and go to sea.
I'd rather feel the sting of strife,
Where gales are born and tempests roar;
Than to settle down to useless life
And rot in dry dock on the shore.
I'd rather fight some mighty wave
With honor in supreme command;
And fill at last a well-earned grave,
Than die in ease upon the sand.
I'd rather drive where sea storms blow
And be the ship that always failed
To make the ports where it would go
Than be the ship that never sailed.

AUTHOR UNKNOWN

Dreaming is a God-given tool. It can lead us far beyond known horizons. Yet dreaming isn't enough. If we long to accomplish great things, we must willingly and courageously do whatever it takes to make our dreams realities. We must never quit while even the most distant glimpse of success remains.

Accomplishing our dreams requires total commitment. To fulfill her dreams, Florence Nightingale pledged her life and herself to a vow still honored in the nursing profession:

"I solemnly pledge myself before God, and in the presence of this assembly, to pass my life in purity and to practice my profession faithfully. I will do all in my power to maintain and elevate the standard of my profession and will hold in confidence all personal matters committed to my keeping and all family affairs coming to my knowledge in the practice of my calling. With loyalty will I endeavor to aid the physician in his work and devote myself to the welfare of those committed to my care."

What do you want to do or be badly enough to make such a commitment?

Jesus had the most daring, far-seeing dream of all when He chose His disciples. Place in the hands of rough, uneducated fishermen, a hated tax collector, and others untrained in public speaking the task of carrying out the salvation of the world?

Preposterous!

But Jesus knew better. Sure, He recognized those men were fallible. He knew they would falter many times, even when they were most needed. But He also knew they possessed an invaluable tool: They had the capacity to rise above their fears and carry out His orders, blessed by His Spirit and strengthened by what they had seen. He had a plan for their lives, even as He has a plan for each of our lives.

Proverbs 29:18 (KJV) says, "Where there is no vision, the people perish." What is your dream, the far-off, seemingly impossible vision that will demand your best until the day you die? Think about it. Pray about it. Make sure your dream is also God's dream for you. Then get started working toward achieving it!

Countless persons set sail into wild and uncharted seas that threaten to swallow them alive. Some become frightened and turn back to safe harbor. Others are blown off their original courses. Those who set their bows to the wind and stick to their original paths find that the dark, seemingly impenetrable clouds often part long enough to permit a reassuring glimpse of the stars. With new resolve, these sailors can redirect their ships toward their goals. Among those who didn't turn back are these outstanding individuals:

- *Robert Bruce,* king of Scotland, once took refuge in a miserable hut, legend says, after losing six battles to free his country from English rule. There he watched a spider swing from beam to beam six times and fail. On the seventh try, it succeeded. Encouraged, Robert Bruce fought again—and won.

- *Henry Wadsworth Longfellow,* poet, experienced no joy on Christmas Day 1863, and for good reason. His son had been wounded in a Civil War battle. But ringing Christmas bells pierced Longfellow's despair and reminded him, "God is not dead, nor doth He sleep." Comforted, he wrote the beautiful, timeless carol, "I Heard the Bells on Christmas Day."

- *A young Dutch boy* who saw water trickling through a hole in the dike is honored by a statue in Haarlem in the Netherlands. No one heard his cries for help, so he bravely plugged the hole with his finger and held back the water until someone came the next day.

- *Louis Braille,* teacher, lost his sight at age three. Instead of focusing on what he could no longer do, he studied hard and later developed the system that has blessed the lives of millions of blind persons.

- *Michelangelo,* artist, is reported to have asked a group of people next to a block of marble what they saw. "A block of stone, you fool," they scoffed. "What do you see?" Michelangelo replied, "I see an angel, imprisoned and waiting to be set free."

- *Walt Disney,* animator and visionary extraordinaire, was supposedly told by the experts he simply couldn't draw and should take up another line of work. Low on funds, he moved into rude surroundings complete with mice. And then one day, he drew one. . . .

- *Christa McAuliffe,* teacher at Concord High School, New Hampshire, began a love affair with space when she was small. In 1984 President Ronald Reagan began a search to choose the first citizen passenger in the history of

America's space program. "A teacher, one of America's finest," he announced. Ms. McAuliffe was selected by NASA from more than 11,000 applicants, reminding us all to "Go for it!"

- *Abraham Lincoln,* president, was determined to serve his country in a public capacity. After several consecutive defeats, Lincoln's friends admonished him to quit what they deemed a lost cause. Lincoln paid no heed to their advice and doggedly continued to pursue his dream. He is now recognized as one of the greatest presidents in the history of the United States of America.

- *Oprah Winfrey,* television host and actress, is a self-proclaimed dreamer. Although she grew up with little money, she knew from a very young age her life would be different. Committed to her dream, she worked hard and at times fought seemingly insurmountable barriers to become the highly successful television personality she is today. Her commitment to her dreams is evident, not only by looking at her career accomplishments, but by the successful battle she has waged against her excess weight. Ms. Winfrey's continued dedication to fulfilling her dreams can be seen by her completion of a marathon.

- *Thomas Carlyle,* writer, lent the sole copy of his hand-written work *The French Revolution, Volume 1* to his friend John Stuart Mill before submitting the book to a publisher. But Mill's maid burned it! Penniless, his notes destroyed, Carlyle penned in his diary, "*It is as if my invisible school master had torn my copybook when I showed it and said, 'No, boy, thou must write it better.'*" Carlyle then proceeded to rewrite the book (published in 1837).

- *Louis L'Amour*, writer, supposedly received two hundred rejections before ever selling anything. He held steady to his course and for several years was recognized as one of the world's top five best-selling authors.

The acronym IRA stands for Individual Retirement Account, a tool that helps ensure a secure financial future. A different IRA can be an even more valuable tool when building a dream.

*I*nspiration from God that your dream is acceptable to Him.
*R*efusal to turn back from the course you (and He) have charted.
*A*ctive, dedicated pursuit of that dream.

After an unsuccessful night of fishing, Simon Peter and his friends wearily obeyed Jesus' command to "Put out into deep water" (Luke 5:4 NIV). They caught so many fish their nets began to break, and the two filled boats began to sink!

Isn't it time for you to leave your comfortable spot on the shore and launch out into deep waters in pursuit of your dream?

PART 4

TOOLS THAT
TAKE YOU TO HEAVEN

God has a unique and perfect plan for every person's life. Discovering what His plan is and carrying it to successful completion takes a lifetime. We need sharp tools to carve out futures that will be pleasing to our Heavenly Father.

One of the best tools God gives us to find our way in this life is the example set by His Son. During His time on earth, Jesus faced every storm, swell, tide, and wave we will ever have to experience. As ancient mariners relied on the North Star for direction, Jesus' example is the beacon by which we can steer our course.

The Scriptures are valuable tools that provide further guidance. Jesus promises:

> *"Let not your heart be troubled:*
> *ye believe in God, believe also in me.*
> *In my Father's house are many mansions. . . .*
> *I go to prepare a place for you. . . .*
> *I will come again, and receive you unto myself;*
> *that where I am, there ye may be also. . .*
> *whither I go ye know, and the way ye know. . . ."*

He then adds:

*"I am the way, the truth, and the life:
no man cometh unto the Father, but by me."*
JOHN 14:1–6 KJV

What is God's greatest dream for us? That we will accept and follow His Son so we may live one day with Them in heaven. All else is secondary. Robert Browning wrote, "My business is not to remake myself, but to make the absolute best of what God made." The following tools help us find and follow the paths by which God would have us return to Him.

1. "DO UNTO OTHERS. . . ."

How we treat others speaks volumes about who we are. Through the centuries, many who have not specifically recognized God *have* realized the importance of treating others well and have provided help on the subject.

- One poem that has stood the test of time is Will Allen Dromgoole's "The Bridge-Builder." It tells of an old man who safely crossed a raging river but stopped at twilight to build a bridge across the chasm. A fellow traveler said, "You'll never come this way again. Why waste your strength?" The old man explained, "A youth followed me today. He will also have to cross in the dim twilight. What was nothing to me, may be a pitfall for him. I build this bridge for him."

*"Whatever you did for one of the least of these
brothers of mine, you did for me."*
MATTHEW 25:40 NIV

- The poem "Not in Vain" describes our true goals in life:

    If I can stop one heart from breaking
    I shall not live in vain;
    If I can ease one life the aching
    Or cool one pain,
    Or help one fainting robin
    Unto his nest again,
    I shall not live in vain.
    EMILY DICKINSON

- An Arabian proverb says if you are ever tempted to
  reveal a tale someone has told you about another, make it
  pass three narrow gates of gold:

    √ The first gate: Is it true?
    √ A narrower gate: Is it needful?
    √ The narrowest gate: Is it kind? If the tale passes
       through the three gateways, you may tell it with-
       out fear of the results.

- James Russell Lowell's magnificent narrative poem "The
  Vision of Sir Launfal" tells of a splendid knight who set

33

forth to find the coveted Holy Grail, the cup from which Christ supposedly drank. Young, proud, and arrogant, he rode forth in all his splendor. Outside the city gate a leper sat, begging alms. Sir Launfal scornfully tossed him a piece of gold and rode on, too intent on his glorious mission to spare time for the loathsome creature.

Weeks became months. Months fled into years. Time and hardship grayed Sir Launfal's hair. At last he turned back, old, sick, ill-clad, and filled with despair. He had found neither the Holy Grail nor the Christ he had sought for a lifetime.

Before entering the city, he paused outside the city gate and noticed a leper seeking alms. Sir Launfal had nothing to give him but a moldy crust of brown bread and water from a wooden bowl. Despite his meager offerings, he gave.

A light shone about the place. The leper that had crouched by Sir Launfal's side now stood before him shining and tall: the Son of God. He bade Sir Launfal not to be afraid, then said,

> "Not what we give, but what we share,—
> For the gift without the giver is bare;
> Who gives himself with his alms feeds three, —
> Himself, his hungering neighbor, and Me."

2. LIVE WORTHY OF HIS NAME.

It is often said Christians are the only Bible some will ever read, the only Christ some will ever see. Our example speaks much louder than words and can be vitally important. Following Christ's teachings and the promptings of the Holy Spirit will help us live worthily and return to Him. We may even bring someone with us.

The Apostle Paul understood the importance of his example when he said:

> *If what I eat causes my brother to fall into sin,*
> *I will never eat meat again,*
> *so that I will not cause him to fall.*
> 1 CORINTHIANS 8:13 NIV

Like Paul, we must recognize that we are tools for God in touching the lives of others. Howard Arnold Walter wrote,

> "I would be true, for there are those who trust me;
> I would be pure, for there are those who care;
> I would be strong, for there is much to suffer;
> I would be brave, for there is much to dare.
> I would be friend of all—the foe, the friendless;
> I would be giving, and forget the gift,
> I would be humble, for I know my weakness,
> I would look up, and laugh, and love and lift."

3. KEEP THINGS IN PERSPECTIVE.

After years of counseling panic-stricken students before key tests, midterms, and finals, a college professor developed a system that appeared to work. He would invite the emotionally distraught collegians to have a seat in his office, then encourage them to explain their feelings. Typically, responses laced with fear, panic, stress, depression, or confusion followed.

The professor would then query, *"If what you are so afraid of were to occur, what is the worst possible thing that could happen?"* After realizing that the worst possible consequences involved failing a single test or doing poorly in a single class (and nothing with significant life impact), most students left without the heavy and overwhelming fears with which they had come. This system worked well for years and resulted in the gaining of perspective and an accompanying reduction of stress for many of his students.

Then came the day that a particularly distraught student expressed that he was feeling an overwhelming sense of fear and panic. The professor asked his usual question. The student replied, "Well, um, I guess I could die." The shocked professor learned the student had been diagnosed with cancer that day. He went home feeling terribly upset about his insensitive and uncaring inquiry. To his surprise, the next day the same student approached him, a smile on his face. Confused, the professor asked why he was smiling.

The student replied, "Facing and verbally recognizing the worst possible thing that might happen really freed me. I realized everyone has to die someday. My energy is no longer consumed by my unidentified fear, but rather with what I must do to live every day I have, the way I want to live."

4. COUNT YOUR BLESSINGS EVERY DAY AND WRITE THEM DOWN IN A JOURNAL AS A REMINDER.

5. DEVELOP AND PRESERVE A CLOSE PERSONAL RELATIONSHIP WITH GOD.

There are those who will attempt to explain to you what God has in store for your life or dictate which path you must follow. The only way to determine whether they are right is to have a personal and close relationship with God. He knows each of us intimately. Because He created us and endowed us with special tools, He knows best how to use those tools. As a carpenter on earth, Christ knew how to effectively use tools to create beautiful pieces of work. When we follow His promptings, He will likewise help us to find and properly use our special tools.

6. DREAM BIG.

In his poem "If," Rudyard Kipling wrote:

> "If you can dream, and not make dreams your master;
> If you can think—and not make thoughts your aim,
> If you can meet with Triumph and Disaster
> And treat those two impostors just the same. . .
> Yours is the earth and everything that's in it. . ."

7. DON'T TAKE YOURSELF *TOO* SERIOUSLY; LAUGHTER IS
   THE BEST MEDICINE.

8. SEEK WISDOM AND ADVICE FROM THOSE YOU ADMIRE.
   Listen to the counsel of those who have lived longer than you. Learn from their mistakes. Experience can often be the best teacher of all.

9. AIM HIGH AND KEEP AN ETERNAL PERSPECTIVE.

> Heaven is not gained at a single bound
> But we build the ladder by which we rise
> From the lowly earth to the vaulted skies,
> And we mount to its summit round by round.

JOSIAH GILBERT HOLLAND (FROM "GRADATIM")

The things of the world often cloud our eternal perspective. In a society measured by the haves and have-nots, it is hard not to succumb to promises of instant gratification and acceptance. Remembering why we are on this journey and where we are headed can help us avoid temptation.

Ralph Waldo Emerson challenged, *Hitch your wagon to a star.*
Jesus commanded us to:

"Seek ye first the kingdom of God, and his righteousness;
and all these things shall be added unto you."
MATTHEW 6:33 KJV

Later Jesus cautioned:

"For where your treasure is, there your heart will be also."
MATTHEW 6:21 NIV

An Eternal Perspective

A young missionary served in a faraway land. After a time, letters from home stopped, leaving him feeling alone and forgotten.

Years later, he sailed home to America. Great crowds stood on shore. *Finally,* he thought, *my work has been recognized.* His heart sank when he realized their cheers were for a popular movie star. Heartsick, the missionary cried, "Why, God? I've spent my whole life serving you. A multitude is giving honor to this idol, but not one person came to welcome me home!"

A still, small voice spoke to his troubled soul.

Peace, my child.
The greatest honors are yet to be given.
You are not yet Home.

Colleen L. Reece of Auburn, Washington, has authored over 100 books, including the best-selling books *Women of the Bible, Apples for a Teacher,* and *A Teacher's Heart,* as well as the popular *Juli Scott, Super Sleuth* Christian teen mystery series. She was voted Favorite Author for *Heartsong Presents* in 1993 and 1994 and inducted into the *Heartsong* Hall of Fame in 1998. More than two million copies of Colleen's books are in print.

Julie Reece-DeMarco is a happily married, practicing attorney in western Washington. A popular guest lecturer, she is often invited to speak to local, state, and national collegiate and professional audiences. Julie's first book, the highly successful *Life 101,* won praise from readers and helped establish the Reece-DeMarco niece-and-aunt writing team.